HOW TO USE THIS LEA...

This leader's guide to *Get Acquainted With Your Christian Faith* provides learning activities for new Christians who are just beginning to explore the Christian faith, as well as those who have been Christians for a long time and who want to better understand the basic tenets of the faith. This guide is designed with the following assumptions:

—adults learn in different ways.
  • by reading
  • by hearing
  • by working on projects
  • by imaginative play
  • by expressing themselves artistically

—the mix of persons in your group is different from that found in any other group.

—the length of your session may vary from thirty minutes to ninety minutes.

—the place where your session is held is not exactly like the place where any other group meets.

—your teaching skills and experiences are unlike anyone else's.

We invite you then to design a unique learning menu for you and your group from the learning idea selections given for each chapter.

—Begin with the Learning Menu headings:

• *As They Enter*: activities that help the group members focus on the theme for the session with introductory activities while they wait for everyone to arrive
• *Learning Idea Selections*: opening and closing devotions, team building activities to build the trust level of the group, and a variety of active ways to experience the major learning goals of the session

• *Bible Background*: additional information on the passages explored in the study book chapter.

—Keeping your group members in mind, choose those learning idea selections that best fit them and your teaching skills. (Try an activity you have not used before. The group members may surprise you.)

—Choose one or more selections for each Learning Menu heading, depending on the length of your session.

No time allowances have been included in the learning idea selections. Every group will take differing amounts of time. You might find it helpful to prepare more learning idea selections than you think you can actually use in the session. But be careful: trying to do too much during one session can be as frustrating as running out of things to do. Be flexible and open to the needs of the group members. This guide is also based on the assumption that the session begins when the first person arrives, so each lesson has some ideas to help individuals focus as soon as they enter the room while they wait for the rest of the group members to gather.

Get Acquainted With Your Christian Faith has an introduction and seven chapters. If you are using the study book and this leader's guide as a resource for a retreat setting or a vacation Bible school study, sessions may be combined, for example, sessions one and two. Omitting one or more entire sessions or rearranging the order of the sessions is not recommended, since the sessions are designed to build on one another to complete the survey of basic Christian beliefs as stated in the statement of faith of the Korean Methodist Church.

INTRODUCTION

Learning Menu

Build your learning menu by selecting one or more learning ideas for each of the Learning Menu headings below:

1. to get acquainted with this study and with one another

2. to explore the Korean Creed as a summary of the Christian faith

3. to experience the difficulty in writing a creed

4. to share faith stories

5. to close the session

AS THEY ENTER

☐A. WORSHIP AREA

—You will need a small table or card table to create a worship center that will change each session. The purpose of the worship table is to provide a focus for the lesson of the day.

—Place a candle and an open Bible in the center of the table. They should remain throughout the study.

—For this introductory session, a copy of the Apostles' Creed and some sports equipment should be prominently displayed on the table.

☐B. DOODLE SHEET

—You will need a large piece of paper and markers.

—In the center of the large piece of paper, write, "I came today because . . ." or "What does a righteous life look like?"

—Tape the paper to a wall, or lay it on a table with some markers nearby.

—As each person arrives, ask him or her to write a first response on the paper.

—As the session begins, place the paper in a prominent place to be referred to later in the session.

LEARNING IDEA SELECTIONS

1. To get acquainted with this study and with one another.

☐A. TAKE A TRIP TO THE BALLPARK

—Ask group members to close their eyes and to imagine they are attending a baseball game. Help their imaginations to smell the hot dogs, taste the popcorn, feel the sun on their back.

—Help them to hear the sounds of the crowd, bats hitting balls, vendors selling their wares.

—Help them to visualize by asking questions like, "Who is playing? Which team is winning?"

—Allow them to enjoy the game for a few minutes.

—Then divide the group members into teams of two or three persons. Discuss: What makes a winning team?

• How do these characteristics apply to your faith?

☐B. WE ARE WHAT WE BELIEVE

—Before the session begins, write "I agree strongly" on one piece of construction paper and write "I disagree strongly" on another piece. Tape these pieces of construction paper at prominent locations on the left and right sides of the room.

—Say: "As the following statements are read, if you agree totally, stand on the side of the room by the 'I agree strongly' sign. If you disagree entirely, stand on the other side. If you are somewhere in the middle, find a position in the room that reflects that opinion."

1. I believe that football is more fun to watch than baseball.
2. I believe that the church's job is to nurture people in the faith.
3. I believe the church's job is to spread the gospel of Jesus Christ.
4. I believe there are too many people dependent on welfare.
5. I believe Jesus' words "as you did it to one of the least of these . . . you did it to me."

6. I believe gun control will only hurt law-abiding citizens, not criminals.

7. I believe we should turn the other cheek when someone hurts us.

8. I believe Jesus died to save me from my sins.

9. I believe that all people are children of God—even atheists.

10. I believe God created the world in seven days.

—Debrief this experience by discussing: How do our beliefs shape the way we live?
  • How do our beliefs influence how we choose our friends?
  • How do our beliefs affect our outlook on life?

☐C. OPENING WORSHIP EXPERIENCE
—Before the session, make small pinpricks in a piece of black construction paper. Be sure the paper is the size of the screen of an overhead projector. Set the projector on a table facing a light-colored wall or a large screen. Put the black paper over the screen of the projector, darken the room, and turn on the projector. Try this ahead of time to be sure the paper is dark enough to block all light except that which comes through the small holes. The effect should be one of an indoor starry sky.
—When all have arrived and are seated, darken the room, turn on the projector, and ask group members to gaze at the sky with all the glittering stars as you read Genesis 15:1-6.
—Ask the group members to spend a few minutes quietly contemplating the magnitude of the promise God made to Abram.
—Then offer a prayer of thanks to God for making us part of Abram's family.

☐D. DISCUSS WHAT THE GROUP MEMBERS EXPECT FROM THIS STUDY
—If you asked group members to complete the statement "I came today because . . ." on the Doodle Sheet, you may use it as a starting point to help them express their goals for this study.
—Be sure to add any new responses to the Doodle Sheet.
—Keep this sheet for your personal reference over the next seven weeks as you choose activities from this leader's guide to fit the group members' goals as well as your own for this study of the Christian faith.

2. To explore the Korean Creed as a summary of the Christian faith.

☐A. READ TOGETHER THE KOREAN CREED
—Ask group members to turn to the "Statement of Faith of the Korean Methodist Church" in the study book (page 5) and to read it together.
—Pause after each sentence to ask if there are any questions or if anyone does not agree with the statement.
—Explain that each of the remaining sessions of this study will focus on a portion of the creed.

☐B. COMPARE THE KOREAN CREED TO THE APOSTLES' CREED
—Compare the Apostles' Creed found on page 4 of the study book with the Korean Creed (page 5). Discuss: What are the strong points of each creed?
  • What are the weaknesses?
  • Which creed do you prefer? Why?

3. To experience the difficulty in writing a creed.

☐A. WRITE A CREED
—You will need paper and pens or pencils.
—Give each group member a sheet of paper and a pen or pencil. Ask members to list five things that they believe about God, love, and/or the meaning of life.
—After an appropriate length of time, explain that they have just begun to write their own personal creed.
—Then form the group members into teams of two or three persons. Ask them to work together to create a creed for their group. They will need to combine their lists of beliefs into one list. When the combined list is completed, it may be converted into a creed by creating statements that begin with "We believe . . ." For example, "We believe that God is love." "We believe that God created the world."
—Ask members to make a clean copy of their joint creed and to sign the creed. Explain that the creeds will be used later in the session.
—Discuss: Where was it easy to agree on your faith statements?
 • At what points did it become difficult to reach a consensus?
(NOTE: Be sure, also, to save these creeds for use during the final session of this study.)

☐B. STUDY THE SHEMA (shuh-MAH)
—You will need a Bible for each group member.
—Ask group members to read Matthew 22:37-39.
—Explain that this is an attempt on Jesus' part to summarize the faith.
—Discuss: How does this passage apply to your life?
 • What is the hardest part of it to keep?
—Then turn to Deuteronomy 6:4-5 and read it aloud.
—Give some background about the importance of this verse (the Shema) to the Jewish faith (see "Bible Background," page 8 of this leader's guide).
—Ask: How is this passage similar to and different from Jesus' faith statement?

4. To share faith stories.

☐A. WHAT DOES FAITH LOOK LIKE?
—Divide the group members into teams of two or three persons. Discuss: What does faith look like?
—Make a list of some faithful people who have inspired the lives of group members.
—If you have used the question "What does a righteous life look like?" on the opening Doodle Sheet, you can use it for a starting point.
—Look up the definition of *righteous* in a dictionary.
—List some examples of righteous people in our world today.
—Discuss: Can you be righteous and faithful without being a Christian?

☐B. COMPARE SOME OF THE WORLD'S RELIGIONS
—You will need copies of the chart on page 7 for each group member.
—As a group, compare some of the other world religions—Judaism, Hinduism, Islam—with Christianity. (See chart, page 7.)
—Ask: What do these religions share, and how do they differ?
—You may also use a video on world religions if one is readily available.

☐C. FIND FAITH IN THE NEWS
—You will need the front page section of old copies of your local news-paper. Try to have enough copies so each group member has one.
—Ask group members to go through the news with an eye to faith.
   • Where do they see faith and values in action?
   • Where in the news is there an absence of faith?
—After an appropriate length of time, ask group members to share headlines of stories that reveal faith in action or the absence of faith.
—Ask group members to keep an eye out for faith in the news during the coming week and to bring examples with them to the next session.

5. To close the session.

☐A. READ A PSALM ANTIPHONALLY
—You will need copies of Psalm 27 for each group member.
—Divide the group members into two groups.
—Read Psalm 27 antiphonally beginning with one group reading the first verse of the psalm and the second group reading the second verse. Ask them to continue to read alternate verses throughout the psalm.
—Or, read the psalm antiphonally by having the women read the first verse, the men the second, and so forth.

☐B. SING A HYMN
—You will need the creeds written earlier in the session. (Note: If you did not choose this menu option, you may want to sing or read the words to the hymn "Lord, I Want to Be a Christian" as a closing prayer.)
—Turn to the words of "Lord, I Want to Be a Christian" in the study book (page 7).
—As group members sing the hymn, ask them to place their signed creeds on the worship table one by one.
—Be sure to collect these creeds after the session and to save them to reuse in Session 7.

☐C. PRAY SILENTLY
—If you used the overhead projection of the starry sky, you may again darken the room and turn on the projector.
—Ask the group members to think about the magnitude of God's love and the enormity of God's creation and in their own hearts give thanks for the gift of faith God has given them.

SOME KEY FACTS ABOUT MAJOR WORLD RELIGIONS[1]

RELIGION	WHERE	SUPREME BEING	FOUNDER/ WHEN FOUNDED	SACRED WRITINGS	TYPICAL HOLY DAYS
Christianity	Europe Western Hemisphere Africa	God	Jesus A.D. 30	Bible New Testament Old Testament	Christmas Good Friday Easter
Islam	Arabia Middle East Africa	Allah	Mohammed A.D. 570–632	Koran	Ramadan (Sacred month)
Hinduism	India Sri Lanka	Brahman/ All Reality	No historical founder 3200 B.C.	Vedas Brahmanas Upanishads Great Epics	The Mela Holi Festival Dasera Divuli
Buddhism	China Japan India Myanmar (Burma)	108 different names	Gautama 560–480 B.C.	Dharma (Sutta) Vinaya Abhidhamma	Perahera Festival in Ceylon (Sri Lanka) Wesak (Kason) in May
Judaism	Israel Europe Western Hemisphere	Yahweh (God)	Abraham 1900 B.C.	Torah Talmud	Rosh Hashanah Yom Kippur Hanukkah Purim Passover

BIBLE BACKGROUND

Genesis 15:1-6

God's call to Abram is the beginning of the covenant that God has continued to make with humankind. Despite our unfaithfulness, God has continued to be faithful. When God saw that the law was too much for humanity to handle, that there was no one who could live without sin, God sent the Son to teach us and save us. This relationship of love and forgiveness we have with God began with Abram and Sarai who said yes when God asked them to venture out into the unknown, to leave everything and everyone they knew to go to some unknown destination that God would ordain. Because these two were willing to risk, God began a long history of reaching out toward humanity.

This passage is the third time in Genesis that God promises to reward Abram with many children. In Genesis 12:1-2, Abram is challenged by God to leave his home and to set out for an unknown destination. In return God promises to make the childless Abram the father of "a great nation." Abram begins his journey in faith; and it leads him out of Haran, through Shechem, down into Egypt, and then back to Bethel where he divides the land with his nephew Lot. Abram generously gives Lot first choice; and Lot chooses the fertile plain of Jordan, which extends from twenty-five miles north of the Dead Sea to the Dead Sea basin itself. Abram and Sarai then travel south and settle in Hebron, claiming the rest of Canaan as God's gift.

God again speaks to Abram in Genesis 13:15-16, affirming his promise of "offspring like the dust of the earth." In Genesis 15, God affirms his promise a third time, even though Abram is growing older and has no heirs. Despite his age, Abram believes God's promise; and because he can still believe, God counts that as righteousness.

There have been many centuries of debate on Genesis 15:6: "and the LORD reckoned it to him as righteousness." It plays nicely into Paul's theory of justification by faith, for Abram had no set of laws or commandments to follow in order to please God. All he had to do was believe. But for centuries theologians have wrestled with the issue of whether faith was a "work" that Abram completed in order to win God's favor or whether even his faith was a gift from God. (To explore this gift versus works issue further, check Romans 4.)

Matthew 22:37-39; Deuteronomy 6:4-5

An old Jewish story tells of the Rabbi Hillel, who lived about two thousand years ago. Supposedly a pagan challenged Hillel that he would become a believer if Hillel could teach him the Torah while the pagan was standing on one foot. Hillel accepted the challenge and said, " 'The law is this: Don't do anything to your neighbor that you don't want anybody to do to you. The other holy laws give you details about how to carry out that most important rule. Now, why don't you go and study?' " And that is just what the pagan did.[2]

Condensing all the laws and commandments into a short, memorable passage was a challenge Jesus quickly accepted. In this Matthew passage, Jesus was answering one in a string of questions posed by the Pharisees and Sadducees to trap him and to disgrace him in front of his followers. Knowing how important the law was to the Pharisees and Sadducees, Jesus recited from the great Shema (Deuteronomy 6:4-5): "You shall love the LORD your God with all your heart, and with all your soul, and with all your might." *Shema* means "hear," and so this passage begins with "Hear, O Israel."

The Shema is the fundamental statement of the Jewish faith, and it is to be pronounced daily by all adult Jews. This prayer is inscribed on a mezuzah (muh-ZOO-zuh), a piece of parchment rolled up in a decorative container and posted on Jews' door frames, so that they are reminded of God's goodness when they go out and come in. This passage is also placed in little boxes that orthodox male Jews wear on their head and wrists to pray. These are called *phylacteries* (figh-LAK-tuh-reez).

The Pharisees and Sadducees could not question Jesus on this response without putting in question their own law that they treasured so dearly. So in essence, Jesus stopped them in their tracks by showing his own knowledge of the Hebrew law. But Jesus, like Hillel, took this prayer one step further in his summary of the faith. He added a horizontal dimension to faith by combining this familiar prayer with Leviticus 19:18: "You shall love your neighbor as yourself." Jesus was affirming that faith in God is central to the faith but so is our treatment of one another.

---

1 Adapted from *The ABC's of World Religions: A Scriptographic Booklet*, by Channing L. Bete Co., South Deerfield, Massachusetts, 1971.

2 From *One Minute Jewish Stories*, adapted by Shari Lewis (Dell Publishing Company, 1989); pages 28–29.

CHAPTER 1

GOD CREATES US

Margaret Preston (1875–1953)
Adam and Eve in the Garden of Eden 1950
gouache stencil on black paper, 50.1 x 49.5 cm.
The Art Gallery of New South Wales

Learning Menu

Build your learning menu by selecting one or more learning ideas for each of the Learning Menu headings below:

1. to experience the process of creating and to reflect on God as Creator

2. to expand our image of God

3. to explore some of the questions surrounding the Creation story

4. to explore our responsibility in our relationship with God as Creator

5. to explore our relationship with God

6. to close the session

AS THEY ENTER

☐A. WORSHIP AREA
—On the worship table, pile stones on top of one another for an altar. These stones should be large enough to write a word on, and there should be enough stones for each group member to have one. Surround this altar with symbols from nature (leaves, flowers, seeds, nuts, and so on), as well as a Bible and a candle.

☐B. DOODLE SHEET
—You will need a large piece of paper and markers.
—Before the session begins, write "I Am Who I Am" in the center of the large piece of paper.
—As persons arrive, ask them to write the name for God that means the most to them on the paper, around the words already there.

☐C. DEBRIEF LAST WEEK'S ASSIGNMENT
—Ask if anyone has brought newspaper headlines describing faith in action.
—Discuss: What ways did you see faith in action during the past week?

LEARNING IDEA SELECTIONS

1. To experience the process of creating and to reflect on God as Creator.

☐A. OPENING DEVOTIONS
—You will need modeling clay.
—Tell group members that *Creator* is one of the most popular names for God. Then explain that there are two types of creators—those who have a plan first and then make their medium correspond to their vision and those who manipulate their medium until an idea emerges and then form a vision from that.
—Give each person a piece of clay. Then form two groups, according to the preferred method of creating.
—As the two groups create something with their clay, ask them to discuss: What are some things you have created during your lifetime?
 • What type of creator do you think God is?
—Then ask group members to imagine all the things God has created with detail and uniqueness such as:
  • the number of wings on a dragonfly
  • the tiny toes of a newborn baby
  • the stripes on a zebra
  • the spots on a giraffe's neck
  • the redwood tree and the tiniest plant
—Ask group members to name other amazing things God has created as they continue working with their clay. List these things on a chalkboard or large piece of paper.
—When group members are finished creating, offer a prayer of thanks to our Creator for all good things.
—Be sure to let group members share what they created before moving on.

☐B. SHARE A STORY
—Check your local library for a copy of *God's Trombones*, by James Weldon Johnson (Viking Press, 1927; Viking Penguin, 1976).
—Read to the group members his poetry sermon called "The Creation" or the portion of the poem printed below.

Then God walked around,
And God looked around
On all that he had made.
He looked at his sun,
And he looked at his moon,
And he looked at his little stars;
He looked on his world
With all its living things,
And God said: I'm lonely still.

Then God sat down—
On the side of a hill where he could think;
By a deep, wide river he sat down;
With his head in his hands,
God thought and thought,
Till he thought: I'll make me a man!

Up from the bed of the river
God scooped the clay;
And by the bank of the river
He kneeled him down;
And there the great God Almighty
Who lit the sun and fixed it in the sky,
Who flung the stars to the most far corner of the night,
Who rounded the earth in the middle of his hand;
This Great God,
Like a mammy bending over her baby,
Kneeled down in the dust
Toiling over a lump of clay
Till he shaped it in his own image;

Then into it he blew the breath of life,
And man became a living soul.
Amen. Amen.[1]

—Then turn to the Creation story in Genesis 1:1–2:4a, and compare it with Johnson's poem.
—Discuss: What similarities do you notice?
  • What differences?
  • Which Creation story makes God seem more personal?

2. To expand our image of God.

☐A. EXPLORE BIBLICAL IMAGES OF GOD
—Using the "Doodle Sheet" as a starting point, explore some of the images of God group members wrote.
—Then read as many of the following list of Scripture passages as time permits, and add any new images of God to the "Doodle Sheet."

Deuteronomy 32:18	Isaiah 42:14	Matthew 6:9	1 John 1:5
Psalm 23:1	Isaiah 64:8	2 Corinthians 3:17	1 John 4:8
Psalm 40:17	Isaiah 66:13	Hebrews 12:29	Revelation 15:3
Psalm 84:11			

—Discuss: Which of these images mean the most to you?
  • Which are hard for you to accept?
—Remind the group members that all names for God are merely metaphors and none is more important than another.
—Close by reading Exodus 3:13-14 and John 4:24.

☐B. CREATE A REMINDER
—You will need toothpicks and tempera paint.
—Give each group member one of the stones from the worship table.
—Ask group members to write their favorite name for God on the stone, using a toothpick and tempera paint.

---

[1]"The Creation," from *God's Trombones* by James Weldon Johnson. Copyright 1927 The Viking Press, Inc., renewed © 1955 by Grace Nail Johnson. Used by permission of Viking Penguin, a division of Penguin Books USA

—Remind them that according to the psalmist in Psalm 18:2, God is our Rock.

—Ask group members to share their names for God and to explain briefly why these names are important to them.

—Suggest that they take their rock home and put it in a prominent place to remind them of this name for God.

3. To explore some of the questions surrounding the Creation story.

☐ A. DISCUSS SCIENCE AND CREATIONISM

—Form group members into teams of two or three persons.

—Ask teams to discuss the following questions about the Creation story: How do you reconcile scientific evidence of dinosaurs and evolution with the Creation story?

• How does your answer affect your understanding of God as Creator?

☐ B. BRAINSTORM QUESTIONS FOR GOD

—Ask group members to pretend they are reporters at a press conference interviewing God about the Creation. What questions would they ask?

—List their questions on a large sheet of paper.

—Then try to answer some of the questions.

☐ C. LEARN ABOUT FRANCIS OF ASSISI AND CREATION

—Read the quotation from Francis of Assisi, page 11 in the study book.

—These words are from the hymn "All Creatures of Our God and King." If copies are available, group members may enjoy singing the hymn or reading the words in unison.

—Check your church or public library for a video or filmstrip on the life of Francis of Assisi. If all else fails, the children's section of your local library may have a biography with pictures. No doubt, whatever you find will accent Francis's love for creation and his belief that he could see God in all the beauty of the world.

4. To explore our responsibility in our relationship with God as Creator.

☐ A. MAKE A COLLAGE

—You will need a large sheet of posterboard, some magazines that can be cut up, scissors, and glue.

—Divide a piece of posterboard in half. On one side write, "Ways we care for God's creation"; on the other write, "Ways we fail to care for God's creation."

—Using the magazines, ask group members to create a double collage of ways we are and are not caring for God's creation.

—Then discuss: Which side was easiest to fill?

• What does this say about our relationship with God?

☐ B. DISCUSS OUR RESPONSIBILITY FOR CREATION

—Discuss: Where can we see God still at work creating?

• How are we a part of that creation?

• Do we take that responsibility seriously? Why or why not?

• If we did take our responsibility seriously, what would the world look like?

□C. MAKE AN ASSIGNMENT
—Ask group members to find ways to be co-creators with God during the coming week.
—If members are keeping a journal, they will want to make a note of how it felt to be a co-creator.
—Ask them to bring their notes to next week's session.

5. To explore our relationship with God.

□A. WRITE A POEM
—You will need pens or pencils and paper.
—Read the story from *Chicken Soup for the Soul*, page 14 of the study book.
—Say: "We are going to look beneath the surface at ourselves and God by writing 'Listing Poems.' A Listing Poem is a group of sentences that begin with the same phrase. In this case you will use 'I am . . .' as the starting phrase and list as many things about yourself as you can think of, each beginning a new sentence."
—The progression in this activity usually goes from shallow observations like "I am thirty years old" to more insightful reflections such as "I am a person who feels things deeply." So encourage the group members to continue after the first one or two sentences.
—After an appropriate length of time, ask those who are willing to share their poems.
—Discuss: Is who you are affected by your faith in God and who you understand God is?
—As a group, write a Listing Poem of all the qualities you know about God, starting with the phrase "God is . . . ."

□B. REFLECT ON BEING A SPIRITUAL BEING
—Ask a group member to read aloud the statement in the margin on page 16 of the study book.
—Discuss: What does it mean to be "a spiritual being having a human experience"?
 • In light of all God has created, what responsibility do we have?

6. To close the session.

□A. READ A PSALM
—Read Psalm 8 as a "sound around"—one person reads the first line; on the second line another person joins in with him or her; on the third line another person joins them. Continue adding voices until everyone is reading the psalm together by the end.

□B. SING A HYMN
—Sing together "How Great Thou Art." The words can be found on page 17 of the study book.

□C. CREATE A PRAYER
—Ask group members to state something for which they are grateful.
—List their responses on a large piece of paper.
—When everyone has contributed, read each item in an attitude of prayer.
—Ask group members to respond to each item with the words "Thank you, Creator God."

BIBLE BACKGROUND

Genesis 1:1–2:4a

This passage is one of the most beautiful stories in the Bible. But it is important to remember that it is a story. Saying that does not mean that it is untrue. In fact, quite the contrary. Stories can be filled with truth and grace. Truth may lie in the meaning of the story as well as the events described.

God created the world we see out of nothing. Whether you prefer the theories of evolution and the Big Bang of science or the story of the creation of the world in seven days as found in Genesis, the bottom line is that God was the primary mover who made all things happen. Someone had to give the push to start things growing and evolving. Someone had to think of all the varieties and details of millions of creatures and plants. All the beauty we see around us could not possibly be the result of a coincidence.

The Creation story that we read in Genesis 1:1–2:4a was transmitted by word of mouth for centuries before it was finally recorded in the form we have it. Like all oral tradition, it was subject to change and embellishment. Every culture has such creation stories, and most of them are so old they can no longer be traced in human history. Light as the first creation of God is also found in the Indian, Greek, and Phoenician traditions. In the Babylonian tradition the world was created by the God of the Sun, Marduk.

Note that this is one of two Creation stories in Genesis from two distinct traditions. The unknown author of Genesis 1 is commonly referred to as "P." The second version begins in Genesis 2:4b with the familiar Adam and Eve story. This story comes from the "J" tradition—a different author and different story altogether.

In the "P" version the emphasis is on God creating. In this version male and female are created at the same time in the image of God. That image was not meant to be interpreted as male or female but as being distinguished from the other creatures by thought, speech, and spirit. These are the things that would keep humankind striving to be in relationship with God.

Another important aspect of the Creation story of Genesis 1 is that God calls the world good. In many of the early church traditions, such as gnosticism (NOS-tuh-siz-uhm), the world was considered evil; and it was only by removing oneself from the world that one could find salvation. Withstanding the temptations of the world was a part of being faithful to God. Genesis 1, however, is in direct contrast with this prevailing theory. Six times God sees all that God has created and calls it "Good." The "P" Creation story wants the reader to see the world God has created as filled with beauty and wonder and as affirming of God's presence and love. The temptation to sin and evil, as Jesus said, comes from inside us not from outside. According to Genesis 1, humankind was given dominion over all that was created so that we could lovingly care as we strive to be in relationship with its Creator.

Exodus 3:13-14

God is mystery. Although God wants a relationship with us, God does not want us to know all there is to know about God. Even God's name is holy. So when Moses asks who he shall say sent him, God answers with the great "I AM." In Hebrew it is written *YHWH*. Scholars differ on how this term should be translated. Some of the possibilities are: "I am who I am," "I am because I am," "I will be as I will be." The latter gives a future dimension that affirms that God will be for all time. Because God chose to avoid naming Godself, we are left to imagine all that God is. To one person God may be a Rock, to another Father, to another the Source of Light and Peace. All our names for God are metaphors, for God has not named Godself. "I am who I am" is all God wants us to know. It is for us to accept the mystery and to allow ourselves to imagine all that God is.

CHAPTER 2

GOD COMES TO US

Learning Menu

Build your learning menu by selecting one or more learning ideas for each of the Learning Menu headings below:

1. to explore light images for God and Jesus Christ in Scripture

2. to discover who Jesus Christ is

3. to personalize the sacrifice Jesus Christ made for us

4. to understand the meaning of discipleship

5. to close the session

AS THEY ENTER

☐A. WORSHIP AREA
—Arrange different types of crosses and a picture of Jesus on the worship table with the Bible and candle.

☐B. DOODLE SHEET
—You will need a large piece of paper and markers.
—At the top of the large piece of paper, write: "Name or draw a hero you admire."
—Post this piece of paper in a prominent position in your classroom. As each group member arrives, ask her or him to write or draw a response to the direction on the paper.

☐C. DEBRIEF ASSIGNMENT
—Ask group members to tell ways they were able to be a co-creator with God during the past week.
—Discuss: How did it feel when you were working with God?
  • How did this exercise make you more aware of God's presence with you and in you?

LEARNING IDEA SELECTIONS

1. To explore light images for God and Jesus Christ in Scripture.

☐A. SCRIPTURE SEARCH
—You will need copies of the following list of "Light Images in Scripture" and a Bible for each team.

"Light Images in Scripture"

Psalm 27:1	John 9:5
Psalm 119:105	John 12:35-36
Isaiah 60:19-22	James 1:17
John 3:17-21	1 John 1:5-7
John 8:12	Revelation 21:22-24

—Divide the group members into teams of two or three persons. Give each team a copy of the list of "Light Images in Scripture" and a Bible. Ask them to look up as many of the passages as possible in the allotted time and to make a list of what the passages say about God or Jesus Christ as "light."
—After an appropriate length of time, ask the teams to report what they found. If all the passages have not been read, you may want to look at them quickly as a total group.
—Then read John 1:1-18 aloud. Discuss: What does this passage tell us about Jesus Christ as "light"?
  • What does it mean to call Jesus Christ "the light of the world"?

☐B. MEDITATE ON THE LIGHT
—You will need a candle and a candleholder. (You may want to use the one on the worship table.)
—Light the candle, and ask the group members to spend time in quiet reflection gazing into the flame.
—Spend about five minutes in this centering exercise. Then ask:

• What thoughts and images did you have as you watched the flame? (Allow group members who do not wish to share to pass.)

• What do you think it means to call Jesus Christ "the light of the world"?

2. To discover who Jesus Christ is.

☐A. READ "ONE SOLITARY LIFE"
—Turn in the study book to page 20, and read aloud the anonymous story about Jesus as "One Solitary Life."
—Discuss: Do you agree with this author's impression of how Jesus Christ has changed the world? Why or why not?

• How has Jesus Christ changed your world?

☐B. ROLEPLAY A MOVIE SCENE
—Ask for five volunteers to recreate a scene from a popular movie.
—Have one person choose a scene with just two people in it from a favorite movie. This person becomes the "director" and gets to sit on a chair and to direct the action of the scene.
—Two of the other volunteers become the characters in the scene, and the other two are the "sound track."
—Have the director describe the scene to the actors and "sound track" in as much detail as possible.
—Next, the director tells the two actors where to stand, while the two voices of the sound track sit behind them.
—When the director shouts, "Action!" the scene begins. The actors depend on the "sound track" to guide their actions.
—Watch the scene play out. The director may stop the scene at any time to make changes to try to get it "right" with his or her memory.
—Usually this activity gets frustrating quickly as the director's vision is filtered through four other people. When the frustration level reaches the point where it is no longer fun, stop the activity and talk about "God as the playwright image" described in the study book (page 19).
—Discuss: How has God directed creation so that it will reflect God's presence in the world?

• How has God "spoken the world into being" so that it is good?

• How have we as the actors distorted God's original vision?

• How has the presence of Jesus Christ changed the storyline?

3. To personalize the sacrifice Jesus Christ made for us.

☐A. READ "THE SUPREME SACRIFICE"
—Turn to page 24 in the study book, and read the section "The Supreme Sacrifice."
—Discuss: How would you have felt if you had been one of those rescued by this man?

• How would the experience have changed your life?

• How has the fact that Jesus Christ made that same sacrifice for you changed your life?

☐B. DISCUSS A SYMBOL OF SACRIFICE
—You will need paper and pens or pencils.
—Ask group members to choose the type of cross each likes best from the collection of crosses on the worship table.

—Then ask them to draw a picture of that cross.
—When all have finished drawing, ask them to choose a partner and to discuss: What do you think of when you see the cross?
  • Why does this cross mean the most to you?

4. To understand the meaning of discipleship.

☐A. WHAT ARE THE TRAITS OF A HERO?
—Using the Doodle Sheet as a starting point, discuss "Who is your hero?"
—Ask: What about the person do you admire?
  • How does that person compare with Jesus?
  • Are you a disciple? What traits do you have that God could use?
  • Who are the "heroes" who have helped to shape your faith?
Have you ever said thank you?

☐B. REMEMBER A TEACHER
—Turn to page 21 in the study book and read aloud "Remembering a Teacher."
—Discuss: Who have been the influential and life-transforming teachers on your life journey?
  • What qualities did those persons have that influenced you?
  • How have you made these persons aware of their important role in your life journey?
  • When have you served as a teacher, encourager for someone else?

☐C. TAKE A LOOK AT YOUR FUTURE
—You will need paper and pens or pencils.
—Ask group members to project themselves twenty or thirty years into the future and to write an obituary for themselves.
—After an appropriate length of time, discuss the following questions:
  • How would you like to be remembered?
  • Are you living life now as you want to be remembered?
  • How are you showing the world you are a disciple of Jesus Christ?

☐D. PRACTICE DISCIPLESHIP
—Put the name of each group member on a slip of paper, and place the slips in a hat or bowl.
—At the close of the session, ask each person to draw a name. Be sure no one gets his or her own name.
—Ask group members to pray each day this coming week for the person whose name they drew.

5. To close the session.

☐A. READ A PSALM
—Ask a woman in the group to read Psalm 131 aloud softly and slowly as the group members repeat each phrase after her.

☐B. SING A HYMN
—Ask the group members to sing or read together the hymn "O Love, How Deep." (The words are found on page 25 of the study book.)

—Teach the group members the Jesus Prayer: "Lord Jesus Christ,
Son of God, have mercy on me a sinner."
—Pray this prayer together, taking a deep breath and reciting the
prayer as you exhale.
—Tell the group members that this prayer can be used at all times in
all places. Ask them to practice it during the coming week.

BIBLE BACKGROUND

The Gospel of John was the last Gospel to be written. Because it follows its own path, it is not linked with the other three Gospels in the Synoptic tradition. John was the poet of the group, and his purpose in writing was not to write a biography of the man Jesus but to affirm Jesus' divinity. Thus, his selection of stories to include and his arrangement of them varies greatly from the other Gospels. Although some of the most beautiful stories in Scripture come from John—the woman at the well, the raising of Lazarus, the story of Nicodemus—his language is often metaphorical rather than factual.

John 1:1-18 is the prologue to this Gospel and as such summarizes the themes of the entire Gospel:

• that Jesus Christ is the agent of a new creation;

• that he is the light and life of this world; and

• that even though he was rejected and crucified, he was acknowledged as the Messiah by those who believed.

In John 1:1-18, the writer uses two important metaphors for Jesus—*Word* and *Light*. The Greek for *Word* is the male noun "logos" (LOH-gohs). This prologue to John begins, as does Genesis, with "In the beginning . . ." because it was important to John's community that Jesus existed before his birth to Mary, that he was indeed always with and a part of God even at the creation of the world. God spoke the Word into being, and it is through the Word made flesh—Jesus Christ—that all the world shall be saved.

The second image is Jesus as the light of the world. (The word *light* occurs no fewer than twenty-three times throughout John's Gospel.) The fear of darkness is a primal instinct for all of us. It is in the darkness that we fumble around and crash into things. It is in the middle of the night that most crises happen. It is in the darkness that we are alone with our thoughts. And it is in the darkness that evil thrives. The writer of John uses *light* as a metaphor for Jesus because from the beginning of time, Jesus, the light, created order and beauty out of chaos and darkness. Then Jesus came into the world as a flesh-and-blood person (the Word made flesh) as the light of the world and again dispelled the darkness of sin and death. Jesus is still the light of the world today, for with his blood is sealed the new covenant of life everlasting.

CHAPTER 3

GOD EMPOWERS US

Learning Menu

Build your learning menu by selecting one or more learning ideas for each of the Learning Menu headings below:

1. to find some commonplace metaphors to understand the person of the Holy Spirit

2. to explore the fruits of the Holy Spirit

3. to experience the power of the Holy Spirit

4. to begin to discover the guidance the Holy Spirit offers

5. to close the session

AS THEY ENTER

☐A. WORSHIP AREA
—You will need a variety of candles in various shapes and sizes.
—Arrange the candles around the Bible and add the sports equipment used in the Introductory Session.

☐B. DOODLE SHEET
—You will need a large piece of paper and markers.
—Before class time, write in the center of the Doodle Sheet, "I feel the presence of the Holy Spirit when . . ."
—As each group member arrives, ask him or her to think about the Holy Spirit of God and to write on the Doodle Sheet the place or time when he or she feels closest to God.

☐C. DEBRIEF ASSIGNMENT
—Ask group members if they prayed the Jesus prayer throughout the week.
—Discuss: Were some times of the day better for the prayer than others?
  • Did the prayer increase your consciousness of Christ's presence with you every day?
  • If so, did it affect your actions in any way?

LEARNING IDEA SELECTIONS

1. To find some commonplace metaphors to understand the person of the Holy Spirit.

☐A. SEE THE HOLY SPIRIT AT WORK
—Using the Doodle Sheet as a starting point, talk about the Holy Spirit as God's presence in the world.
—Ask: Why does God's presence seem stronger in some places and situations than in others?
  • How can we be more conscious of the Holy Spirit in all times and places?

☐B. REMEMBER A TIME OF COACHING
—Ask the group members to close their eyes and to relax.
—Tell them to take three deep breaths.
—Then ask them to remember a time in their past when they taught, encouraged, or coached someone. Perhaps it was a Little League team or a youth choir or a Sunday school class. Perhaps it was teaching someone how to fix something or to follow a recipe.
—Ask them to recall all the feelings that went with that experience—patience, a positive attitude, frustration.
—As they look back at the experience, could they have done it better? How?
—Then ask them to open their eyes and to return to the present. Allow time for them to share their coaching experiences. What made them good or bad at this task?
—Considering Kent Millard's comparison of the Parakletos (Holy Spirit) with a coach (page 28 of the study book), how does your experience enlarge your understanding of the work of the Holy Spirit?

2. To explore the fruits of the Holy Spirit.

☐ A. IMAGINE FRUITS
—Ask group members to close their eyes and to imagine they are eating a piece of fruit. Tell them that it is the best-tasting piece of fruit they have ever eaten. Allow time for them to enjoy it.
—Guide the meditation with questions like these:
  • Is the juice sweet or tart?
  • As you chew, what texture does the fruit have?
  • Where are you as you enjoy eating this fruit?
—After an appropriate length of time, divide the group members into small teams according to the fruit they were enjoying. If several persons have unique fruits, they may form a team.
—Ask the teams to turn to Galatians 5:22-26 and to decide which of the fruits of the Spirit they think reminds them of the fruit they were imagining. For example, a peach might be like patience because both are delicate and rosy.
—After an appropriate length of time, ask the teams to discuss the following question: Why do you think Paul called these fruits of the Spirit?
—If time permits, ask the teams to share their discussion with the total group.

☐ B. COMPLETE A TALENT INVENTORY
—You will need copies of the "Gifts of the Spirit Talent Inventory" (page 24 of this leader's guide). Add to the inventory activities that are specific to your local church.
—Give a copy of the "Gifts of the Spirit Talent Inventory" to each group member.
—Ask each member to reflect on his or her talents and skills and to fill out the form.
—Allow time for members who wish to share some of their talents and how they could use them for God's glory. (Note: If this is a new members group, encourage everyone to get involved in the church by using this inventory as a tool to find the places they can help the most. Be sure to give information from the inventories to church officials who might have a need for volunteers.)

3. To experience the power of the Holy Spirit.

☐ A. REFLECT ON LIFE
—Ask group members to close their eyes and to think of a place in their life where they need to feel the power of the Holy Spirit—some brokenness or some problem.
—Tell them to quietly ask God for the power of the Holy Spirit in this situation and then to visualize what that will look like.
—After an appropriate length of time, discuss: Did you feel God give you the power you need?
  • If so, how does it feel?

☐ B. WRITE A CINQUAIN
—You will need a large piece of paper, a marker, sheets of paper for each group member, and pens or pencils.
—Ask group members to think of people they know who are filled with the Holy Spirit.

—Discuss: What attributes do these persons have that made you choose them?
  • Do they inspire you to want to increase your faith?
—List on the large sheet of paper some of the characteristics of a life filled with the Holy Spirit.
—Give each group member a sheet of paper, and ask members to write a cinquain (sihn-CANE) describing the work of the Holy Spirit. A cinquain poem has five lines in the pattern below:

Line 1: a noun that serves as title
  one word
Line 2: describes the title
  two words
Line 3: action words (verbs) or a phrase about the title
  three words
Line 4: describes a feeling about the title
  four words
Line 5: a word that means the same thing as the title
  one word

A SAMPLE CINQUAIN

Tolerance
lenient stance
accepting, including, absorbing
accepting you as equal
Inclusivity

If persons have trouble, suggest several work together to create one poem.
—Ask for volunteers to read their poems, and notice how different each is.

□C. READ A PLAY ABOUT THE HOLY SPIRIT
—You will need three copies of the play "The Helper." (See page 25 of this leader's guide.)
—At the beginning of the session assign three women to play the roles of Janie, Suzy, and Mary in "The Helper."
—Ask the other group members to watch the play and to make notes of how the Holy Spirit helps Janie.
—Discuss: Is the Spirit helping in any ways Janie doesn't name?
  • Have you ever talked to anyone about the Holy Spirit or about how God is acting in your life?
—If time permits, roleplay your own scenes of telling someone about the Holy Spirit.

4. To begin to discover the guidance the Holy Spirit offers.

□A. THINK ABOUT COINCIDENCES
—Read together the story of the writer's strange hospital visit from the study book (page 29).
—Discuss: Do you believe this was a coincidence or a movement of the Holy Spirit?
  • Can you name some "coincidences" in your past that have been the leading of the Holy Spirit?
  • Did you recognize them at the time?
  • If not, how might the outcome have changed if you had?
  • How can we be sensitive to the movement of the Spirit? (trusting our own intuition, stopping in crisis to listen for God's voice, grounding ourselves in prayer, practicing the fruits of the Spirit)

□B. EVALUATE THIS SESSION
—Discuss: Where did you feel the power of the Holy Spirit in this session?
  • Is God calling you to anything new?
  • How can we put our spiritual gifts to better use for God?

☐C. MAKE AN ASSIGNMENT
—Ask group members to use intentionally during the coming week the fruits of the Spirit they have acknowledged.

5. To close the session.

☐A. READ A PSALM
—You will need copies of Psalm 23 for each group member.
—Ask group members to read Psalm 23 in unison. Have them begin in a whisper and get louder with each verse until they are shouting at the end.

☐B. SING A SPIRIT SONG WITH MOTIONS
—Sing "Spirit of the Living God" (see page 33 of the study book), using the movements below:
   • Spirit of the Living God—arms up, hands open upward to receive the Spirit
     • Fall afresh on me—hands come down and wash over shoulders
     • Repeat
     • Melt me—bend over from the waist, shoulders sag
     • Mold me—straighten from waist, shoulders still sagging
     • Fill me—straighten shoulders
     • Use me—hands out and open at waist to be used
     • Repeat first two lines

☐C. CLOSE WITH PRAYER
—Ask group members to turn to page 33 in their study book and to pray together "An Invitation to the Holy Spirit."

GIFTS OF THE SPIRIT TALENT INVENTORY

LOVE
—— Visiting current members
—— Serving on child care board of directors
—— Working at the food pantry
—— Being head usher
—— Coordinating receptions after funerals and weddings
—— Helping to serve meals

JOY
—— Greeting on Sunday mornings
—— Being a song leader
—— Singing in the choir
—— Sharing your musical talent
—— Being part of a clown ministry
—— Joining an acting troupe

PEACE
—— Visiting in the hospital
—— Working as a volunteer with a crisis hotline
—— Serving as a lay home visitor to shut-ins
—— Working with Hospice

PATIENCE
—— Teaching in the children's Sunday school
—— Teaching or helping with Vacation Bible School
—— Working with youth group
—— Planting and caring for flowers around the church

KINDNESS
——— Driving shut-ins to church or doctor's visits
——— Typing the church bulletin
——— Delivering Meals on Wheels
——— Being a member of the prayer chain
——— Serving on the local interfaith council
——— Providing a meal for a member of the congregation who is sick

GENEROSITY
——— Working around the church with carpentry, plumbing, and so forth
——— Making Easter eggs
——— Hosting a small group study in your home
——— Working on the church lawn

FAITHFULNESS
——— Serving as worship leader
——— Leading a small group Bible study or prayer group
——— Visiting prospective members
——— Visiting in the neighborhood
——— Serving as evangelism chairperson
——— Volunteering to help with Parent's Night Out

GENTLENESS
——— Leading the church council
——— Editing the church newsletter
——— Serving as a nursery attendant during worship
——— Ushering people to their seats
——— Being a mentor for a confirmand

SELF-CONTROL
——— Raising plants for the plant ministry
——— Auditing the church books
——— Serving as financial secretary or treasurer
——— Serving on the finance committee

THE HELPER[1]

Janie: Have you ever heard of the Holy Spirit?
Suzy: The what?
Janie: The Holy Spirit.
Suzy: No, what is it?
Mary: My mom says you should always be filled with the Holy Spirit.
Suzy: How much do you have to eat before you get full?
Janie: You don't eat it, silly. He's a person, and my dad says He's our helper.
Mary: I haven't seen any Holy Spirit helping me clean my room lately. What kind
     of helper is he if he won't do that?
Janie: I think He's supposed to help us be more like God.
Mary: Does he help with homework?
Janie: I don't think so.
Suzy: Well, how much do you have to pay him for his help?
Janie: You don't pay Him, you must ask Him and then He helps you.
Mary: Really?
Janie: Yep.
Suzy: Can the Holy Spirit help me not hit my brother?
Janie: I think so, but you've got to want to not hit him, too.
Suzy: Oh.
Mary: Well, what about sharing? Can the Holy Spirit help me share my toys? I get
     in so much trouble for being selfish.
Janie: I think He can.

Suzy: Are you sure the Holy Spirit can make people more like God?
Janie: Yeah.
Suzy: Then how come the world isn't a nicer place, huh? How come more people don't act nice, like God?
Janie: Maybe they forget to ask the Holy Spirit for help.
Suzy: Well, when I grow up, I'm going to remember to ask the Holy Spirit to help me be more like God.
Janie: Me too! I'm gonna ask a hundred times a day 'cause I really want to be like Him.
Mary: Well, I'm gonna ask a zillion times a day.
Suzy: Then I'm going to ask a million zillion times a day.
Janie: I don't think we're acting much like God now.
Suzy: I guess it's going to take a while for us to get the hang of this.
Janie: Yeah, so it's a good thing we're starting now.

BIBLE BACKGROUND

John 14:15-17, 25-26

Once Jesus started talking to his followers about his death, they not only refused to believe such a thing could happen but they also could not imagine how they would survive without him. They wanted to continue to sit at Jesus' feet and to witness his miracles and listen to his words. But Jesus knew his time on earth was limited, and so he tried to prepare his followers with passages like John 14. Jesus wanted to assure the faithful then and now that even though he would suffer and die and ascend into heaven, he would not abandon them.

In John 14, Jesus reassures the disciples that when he leaves and his physical presence is not with them anymore, God will send a spiritual presence that will empower them to take over the task of forming his church. Jesus assures them and us that this Spirit of truth will never leave but indeed will abide with them and in them.

Jesus' promise was fulfilled on the day of Pentecost as described in Acts 2. Pentecost was and still is a Jewish holy day. It commemorates for the Jews the first revelation of God in the form of the Ten Commandments, the holy laws that sealed God's covenant with Israel. It was on this special holy day that God chose to again reveal Godself. On the first Pentecost after Jesus' crucifixion, God sent the Holy Spirit to those gathered together in Christ's name; and so Christians celebrate Pentecost also. However, we remember the day as the birthday of the church.

---

[1]From *Three-Minute Dramas for Worship*, by Karen Patitucci (Resource Publications, 1989), pages 143–45.

CHAPTER 4

GOD FORGIVES US

Learning Menu

Build your learning menu by selecting one or more learning ideas for each of the Learning Menu headings below:

1. to understand how the gift of God's grace can change us	2. to reflect on personal guilt and the need for forgiveness	3. to reflect on the need to forgive in order to be forgiven	4. to experience baptism as an act of forgiveness and grace	5. to close the session

AS THEY ENTER

☐A. WORSHIP AREA
—You will need a cross, a bowl or large sea shell of water, and a large piece of paper.
—Place the cross and bowl or sea shell on the worship table, along with the candle and Bible.
—Write the Serenity Prayer on the large piece of paper, and place it on the wall behind the worship table:

"Lord, grant me the serenity to accept the things I cannot change, the courage to change the things I can, and the wisdom to know the difference."

☐B. DOODLE SHEET
—You will need two large pieces of paper and markers.
—Place the two large pieces of paper on the walls at opposite sides of the room. On one write "Sin is . . ." and on the other write "Grace is. . . ."
—As group members arrive, direct them to add a thought to both sheets.

☐C. DEBRIEF ASSIGNMENT
—Form the group members into teams of two or three persons.
—Ask the teams to discuss: How were you able to use your fruit of the Spirit during the past week?
  • Was it difficult to do?
  • Did you discover any other gifts of the Spirit that you can use?
  • When did you observe others using their gifts?

LEARNING IDEA SELECTIONS

1. To understand how the gift of God's grace can change us.

☐A. OPENING DEVOTIONS
—Read the section "We Believe in the Forgiveness of Sins" from the study book (page 35).
—Explain that we all need to take the first two steps of the twelve-step Alcoholics Anonymous program—admit our powerlessness against sin and put ourselves in God's hands. That is why the Serenity Prayer is so popular.
—Pray the prayer together.

☐B. TAKE PART IN AN EXERCISE IN CHANGE
—Ask group members to choose a partner. Then form two lines, with partners facing each other.
—Tell them they have two minutes to study their partner and to get to know him or her without using words.
—At the end of the two minutes, ask the partners to turn their backs to each other.
—Then instruct them to change three things about their physical appearance.
—When everyone has changed three things, ask the partners to face each other again and to see if they can find the three changes.

—Ask: Did you remove something or add something to change your appearance? (Most likely you will find that people took something off as opposed to adding something.)

- What, if anything, does this say about us?
- Was it hard to change three things?
- How hard is it to change our lives?
- When God changes us, do we take off something or add something?
- Was it more difficult to study the person initially or to find the three changes?
- How important is it for us to notice the other person in order to have a relationship?
- How much time do we spend in a day noticing God?

☐C. RECEIVE A FREE GIFT
—You will need a wrapped gift for each group member. It could be something as small as a pencil or something handmade.
—Give each member a gift, saying it is from you to them because you love them.
—Watch, empty-handed, while they open their gifts.
—Allow time for them to enjoy their presents and to give their thanks. Then ask: How did it feel to receive a gift with nothing to give in return?

- Why do you think it is hard for us to accept gifts graciously?
- What does "accepting gifts graciously" mean?
- How does it relate to the word *grace*?

—Using the Doodle Sheets as a starting point, discuss what grace is and how it relates to sin.
—Ask: Is it also hard for us to accept God's grace with nothing to give in return? Why or why not?

☐D. SURRENDER ALL TO CHRIST
—Turn to page 36 of the study book, and read aloud the section "Seeking Forgiveness."
—In pairs, explore the questions in the "Pause for Reflection" on page 37 of the study book.
—After an appropriate length of time, ask each pair to close by praying together for God's guidance and the ability to trust God and surrender all.
—End by blessing one another by making the sign of the cross on each other's forehead and saying, "I bless you in the name of the Father, Son, and Holy Spirit."

2. To reflect on personal guilt and the need for forgiveness.

☐A. DISCUSS HOW GUILT HAS AFFECTED YOUR LIFE
—Form small teams of two or three persons.
—Ask each team to read Romans 5:12-21.
—Then ask them to discuss: What are the implications of Adam's sin and Jesus' grace in light of your own experience?
—Ask them to share some mistakes they have made for which they have received God's forgiveness.
—If the trust level is high enough, tell them they are free to share some of the mistakes for which they do not feel forgiven.
—After an appropriate length of time, have the teams pray for one another's forgiveness.

□B. STUDY "THE EXAMEN"

—You will need copies of "The Examen," page 32 of this leader's guide, for each group member.

—Give each group member a copy of "The Examen." Explain that this is a prayer technique developed by Ignatius of Loyola during the Middle Ages. It has been passed down and revised over the centuries to our generation. This particular version was adapted by Father Edward Sanders, while adjunct professor of Spiritual Nurture at Lancaster Theological Seminary.

—In an attitude of prayer, walk the group members through the five steps, allowing times of silence after each for quiet personal reflection.

—Debrief the experience by asking questions such as: Were you able to list more moments of grace or more moments of sin during the day?

• Were you able to feel God's gentle gift of forgiveness?

• What grace do you think you are being invited to ask for?

—Ask the group members to take this prayer guide home with them and to practice it during the coming week.

3. To reflect on the need to forgive in order to be forgiven.

□A. BIBLE STUDY

—You will need a Bible for each team.

—Form teams of two or three persons.

—Ask the teams to read Matthew 22:36-39.

—Discuss: What does this passage say to you personally?

• Which words or key phrases stick in your mind? Why?

• What does the phrase "love your neighbor as yourself" mean to you?

□B. DISCUSS MICHAEL'S STORY

—Read the section "Offering Forgiveness to Others" from the study book (page 38).

—Discuss: Could you have found it in your heart to forgive Michael as the minister in this story did?

• How do you think that made Michael feel?

• If you were Michael, what change would that kind of forgiveness bring to your life?

• Is there anyone that you are finding it hard to forgive?

• How could you go about forgiving that person?

4. To experience baptism as an act of forgiveness and grace.

□A. DRAW A PICTURE

—You will need paper and markers or crayons.

—Tell the group members that baptism is new birth in Christ. Explain that the water of baptism is not only a symbol of cleansing but also a symbol of birth. (See page 44.)

—Give group members paper and markers or crayons and ask them to draw a picture of what new life in Christ looks like for them.

□B. DO A MEDITATION ON FORGIVENESS

—Lead group members in the following meditation on forgiveness:

Close your eyes and concentrate on relaxing. Take three deep breaths. (Silence)

Now just concentrate on emptying your mind from all the business of the day. Wipe your mind clean, like an eraser over a slate. Concentrate on your body working; listen to your breathing. (Silence)

When you are relaxed, imagine yourself in your favorite spot—a grove of trees, a mountain peak, the ocean shore. Picture that place in your mind, smelling all the smells, tasting the freshness of the air, hearing the comforting sounds of this safe place. (Silence)

Now imagine that you are ten years old and enjoy this place as a child—run and skip and jump. Touch and taste. Enjoy. Feel the sun on your back and the gentle breeze on your cheeks. (Silence)

Now imagine before you a mud puddle, filled with mud to be molded and squeezed and enjoyed. Jump in that puddle. Relax in it. Play in it with carefree abandon. (Silence)

Now you hear the footsteps of an adult. You jump out of the puddle, covered with mud. Your father appears, and suddenly you are filled with guilt and shame. You start apologizing, but your father responds as he normally would in this situation. (Silence)

You feel his displeasure and you yearn to make things right. He takes you by the hand and leads you to a spring of clean fresh water. You jump in clothes and all. He hands you a bar of soap, and you wash yourself clean. And as you wash away the mud, you wash away the guilt as well. (Silence)

Your father smiles at you and helps you to get off the final traces of mud. Then he gives you a hug and tells you he loves you, and you feel good all over.

Your father leaves, and you once again are alone in this favorite place. The sun gently dries your wet clothes and body; the gentle breeze again feels good upon your cheeks. You take a deep breath of clean air and feel the cleanness of your body and your soul. And you smile, for you know you are loved.

Enjoy that moment; and when you are ready, open your eyes and return to this classroom.

5. To close the session.

☐A. GIVE AN ASSIGNMENT
—Give group members a copy of the following "Prayer for Bathing." Ask them to pray it before bathing each day this week.

Blessed are you, Lord God, Creator of all good things
and your Son Jesus Christ, who saves us from our sins
who has made us holy through the water and the Spirit.
O swiftly flowing water, purifying flood, bathe us gently
And cleanse us of our sins this day.
As the dirt and dust is washed away,
Wash away the mistakes we have made today as well.
As the holy water flows over our bodies and spirits,
May we remember the vows made at our baptism
To be followers of Jesus Christ this day and always. Amen.[1]

☐B. CLOSE WITH PRAYER
—You will need copies of the "Prayer for Bathing." (See above.)
—Close the session by praying the "Prayer for Bathing" in unison as group members dip their hands in water.
—Or, use the Serenity Prayer. (See page 28.)

1. Ask Christ, Light of the World, to walk with you through the day.
2. Thank God for specific gifts of the day.
3. Celebrate God's empowering love at those moments of the day when you were loving or loved.
4. Celebrate God's undefeated love at those moments when you were less than loving. "I know that *and* I love you."
5. What grace am I being invited to ask for? What would life look like if grace were given?

BIBLE BACKGROUND

Matthew 6:9-15

Learning how to pray is one of the most important tasks for a new Christian. Getting to know God on a personal basis requires setting aside time to commune with and communicate with God. How to pray and for what to pray are also of great concern to growing Christians. And they were a concern to Jesus' first followers. In Matthew 6, part of Jesus' Sermon on the Mount, he attempts to instruct the crowd on how to live a godly life and how to pray. Jesus warns them against praying in public just to be seen, for he says those folks have already received their reward (verse 5). Jesus also advises, "Do not heap up empty phrases" that may sound beautiful but have little meaning for you. God knows our needs even before we ask, and God is not fooled by phony displays or fancy words (verses 7-8).

Then Jesus gives us a guide for our prayer life (verses 9-13). This prayer is just a guide, for our prayers should be from our hearts and experiences. He begins by telling us it is all right to address God as a parent, for God has created us and loves us as a parent. God is not some distant ruler on a heavenly throne; God is as close to us as a parent—waiting, wanting to hear our concerns and to help us. The fact that Jesus uses the plural pronoun in "Our Father" affirms that we are a community, a family of faith, and that we are never alone, even in our prayer times.

The rest of this model prayer follows a formula of praise, submission, petition.

praise—"Hallowed be your name."

submission—"Your kingdom come. / Your will be done, / on earth as it is in heaven."

petitions: give us bread to meet our physical needs

forgiveness to bring our souls into right relationship with God and one another

protection from the temptations that surround this earthly existence.

Jesus also adds a warning about asking for forgiveness. We can expect God's forgiveness, but we must be equally willing to forgive those who seek our forgiveness.

Romans 5:12-21

Paul's Letter to the Romans is different from his other letters in that this is the only community that he had not visited and preached to personally. Because he had not met them and spoken to them, this letter presents the most fully developed statement of Paul's theology. He wanted to be sure that he covered all the important aspects of the faith for them.

One of these basic tenets is revealed in Chapter 5. How sin came into God's beautiful, perfect creation was of great concern to Paul. He could not ascribe sin to God's plan; therefore, it must have entered the world through the human error of Adam and been inherited by each subsequent generation. Paul saw Christ as the New Adam, who had come to right the world and to restore our loving relationship with God.

God offers us this free gift—a gift we call grace. We cannot do anything to earn it, for Jesus has already suffered for us and borne the punishment for our sin. We are justified or made right through Christ. All we need to feel God's forgiveness is to believe in Jesus Christ and his sacrifice for us.

---

1 Adapted by Suanne Williams-Whorl from a suggestion in *In Pursuit of the Great White Rabbit*, by Edward Hays (Forest of Peace Books, 1990).

CHAPTER 5

GOD INSTRUCTS US

Learning Menu

Build your learning menu by selecting one or more learning ideas for each of the Learning Menu headings below:

1. to explore the Bible as God's road map

2. to explore some new ways to understand the Bible

3. to see the Bible as a way to transform lives

4. to close the session

AS THEY ENTER

☐ A. WORSHIP AREA
—You will need a road map and if possible a copy of *Life's Little Instruction Book*.
—Place the road map and copy of *Life's Little Instruction Book* on the worship table, along with the Bible and candle.

☐ B. DOODLE SHEET
—You will need a large piece of paper and markers.
—Before the session, write your favorite Bible verse in the center of the Doodle Sheet.
—As group members arrive, direct them to the Doodle Sheet; and ask them to add their favorite Bible verse to yours.

☐ C. DEBRIEF ASSIGNMENT
—Discuss: Which of the two prayers from last week's session ("The Examen" or "The Prayer for Bathing") were you able to use regularly this past week?
  • Did the prayer or prayers help you in any way?
  • Was it easier for you to forgive or to feel forgiven?
  • How could you adapt either of these prayers to a form you would use daily?

LEARNING IDEA SELECTIONS

1. To explore the Bible as God's road map.

☐ A. OPENING DEVOTIONS
—Read 2 Timothy 3:14-17. End with the closing "This is the Word of God; Thanks be to God."
—Ask: What does the Bible mean to you?
—Close with prayer, asking God to enlighten the group through God's Word.

☐ B. GO ON A TREASURE HUNT
—You will need several small objects suitable for hiding in the church and lists of the objects for each search party.
—Hide the small objects in the church building before the session.
—Form the group members into search parties of three or four persons.
—Give each group a list of the objects, and tell them the objects are hidden somewhere in the church building.
—Give the group members five minutes to search and regather.
—When all have returned to the classroom, celebrate if any of the objects have been found.
—Then give each search party a map of the church with the hidden items marked on it, and ask them to search again for five minutes.
—When all the search parties have returned to the classroom, ask: Which way was easier to find what you were looking for?
—Tell the group members that the Bible is our road map. It helps us find meaning on life's journey.

☐ C. MAKE AN INSTRUCTION BOOK
—You will need paper and pens or pencils and a copy of *Life's Little Instruction Book* if available.

—Read some excerpts from *Life's Little Instruction Book*. If you do not have a copy, use the ones listed on page 46 of the study book.
—Discuss: Which of these "instructions" mean the most to you?
 • Which ones would you like to pass on to children or grandchildren?
—Then read some of the Bible's instructions. (See the "Pause for Reflection" on page 49 of the study book.)
—Ask: Which of these instructions are easiest to follow?
 • Which are more difficult?
—Using these two sets of instructions as examples, ask the group members to write some notes for children or grandchildren from their life experience or tradition.
—After an appropriate length of time, give those who are willing an opportunity to share their instructions.
—Ask: How many of these are based on stories or instructions found in the Bible?

2. To explore some new ways to understand the Bible.

☐A. PRACTICE THE *LECTIO DIVINA* APPROACH TO BIBLE STUDY
—You will need Bibles and copies of "The *Lectio Divina* (LEK–shee–oh dih–VEE–nah) Approach to Bible Study," page 37 of this leader's guide.
—Form the group members into teams of three or four persons.
—Ask the teams to open their Bibles to 2 Timothy 3:10-17 and to read the passage aloud at least twice, using different readers. Have them listen attentively to what God may be telling them through these biblical words.
—After the reading, ask them to discuss: What message do you think God is trying to give you right now through this passage? (Explain that part of the power of Scripture is to give us the message we need at the right time.)
 • What is your reaction to that message?
 • How can you apply that message in your everyday lives?
—Explain that the method of Bible study that you have been using is called "*Lectio Divina*." Give each group member a copy of "The *Lectio Divinia* Approach to Bible Study" (see page 37 of this leader's guide). Suggest that they practice this method during the coming week.
—Ask everyone to join hands in their teams and to spend a few moments together in silent prayer.

☐B. DO SOME BIBLE RESEARCH
—You will need a Bible, a concordance, a Bible atlas, a Bible dictionary, and at least one Bible commentary. You may borrow these from your pastor or church library.
—Read John 8:1-11.
—Form the group members into four teams. Explain that each team will research a different aspect of the story, using the resource books you have brought.
—Assign teams as follows:
 • Team One will locate Jerusalem and the Mount of Olives on a map.
 • Team Two will use the Bible dictionary to learn who the Pharisees were.
 • Team Three will look up the word *adultery* in the concordance and explore several of the passages listed.
 • Team Four will use the commentary to gain additional information about the passage.

—Give the teams fifteen minutes for their research. Then call everyone together to share their findings.
—Ask: How do these facts make the story clearer?

3. To see the Bible as a way to transform lives.

☐A. PRACTICE THE IGNATIAN CONTEMPLATION APPROACH TO BIBLE STUDY
—You will need copies of "The Ignatian Contemplation Approach to Bible Study," page 37 of this leader's guide, for each group member.
—Ask the group members to turn in their study books to "Shaped by the Word," page 50, and to read the author's account of his experience with John 8:1-11.
—Tell the group members that you are going to read the story three times. Each time they are to close their eyes and try to place themselves in the story in the person of one of the characters—the woman, her accusers, a bystander, Jesus. Ask them to change characters each time the story is read.
—Following the readings, form the group members into pairs or teams of three persons to discuss: What characters did you become in the story?
  • What insights did you gain from looking at the story from different points of view?
  • Is this a valid method of studying the Bible that you could use at home? Why or why not?
—Explain that this method of Bible study is known as "Ignatian Contemplation." Distribute copies of "The Ignatian Contemplation Approach to Bible Study," page 37 of this leader's guide. Suggest that group members practice this method of Bible study during the coming week.

☐B. CREATE A COLLAGE
—You will need enough recent newspapers and magazines for each group member to have one, a large circle cut from a piece of blue posterboard, and scissors.
—Give a recent newspaper or magazine to each group member.
—Ask them to look through the magazine or newspaper for signs of brokenness and lostness.
—Have the group members cut out these articles or pictures and paste them on the large circle (representing the world) cut from the piece of blue posterboard.
—As they cut and paste, encourage group members to share their discoveries with one another.
—When they are finished, ask: How can God's Word help transform our world?
  • What can we do to start that process happening?

4. To close the session.

☐A. GIVE AN ASSIGNMENT
—Ask the group members to study one passage a day during the coming week, using the Lectio Divina or Ignatian Contemplation approach (see page 37 of this leader's guide).
—Texts used in next week's lesson are: Matthew 16:13-18; Matthew 25:31-45; Acts 2; 1 Corinthians 12; and Ephesians 2:19-20.

☐B. READ A HYMN
—Join group members in reading the words of the hymn "O Word of God Incarnate," page 53 of the study book.

The *Lectio Divina* Approach to Bible Study

(Each of the four steps should be accomplished at each sitting on the same passage of Scripture. Some steps may take longer than others. Be sensitive to which steps require more attention on any given day or passage.)

1. Listen attentively to what God is telling you in the words of Scripture by trying to read between the lines to discover the deeper meaning.
2. Reflect prayerfully upon this deeper meaning and try to apply it to your life situation.
3. Respond to God's word by appropriate feelings and actually create a dialogue with God, openly stating how you feel and waiting respectfully for any answers.
4. Remain quiet and still in order to be open to any new insights.

The Ignatian Contemplation Approach to Bible Study

1. Read the passage over from beginning to end.
   A. Pay particular attention to details—where, when, how, why, and so forth.
   B. List the characters involved—how many are there, what might they look like, and so forth.
2. Do you have a sufficient understanding of the story to visualize it, or do you need to read it again?
3. Close your Bible, set the scene in your mind—picture the time of day, the colors involved, the smells, and so forth.
4. Put yourself into the scene in whatever role or position you feel comfortable.
5. Play out the scene drawing on all the details you remember from the reading and improvising the rest.
6. Continue meditating on the passage until you feel comfortable leaving it, then return to the present.
7. Reflect on, possibly journaling, what happened and what impact it had on you. Did you receive any new insights into what the characters were thinking or feeling? What does this passage have to say to you and your life right now?[1]

BIBLE BACKGROUND

John 8:1-11

One of the reasons this particular story was chosen for study is because it hearkens back to Chapter 4 and the need for us to be able to forgive others in order to receive God's forgiveness. The woman in John 8 was a sinner and according to the Hebrew law was deserving of the stoning that she was about to receive. But, Jesus stepped in and pointed out that no matter how righteous we think we are, we have all sinned before God. Therefore, forgiveness is a necessity in the church of Jesus Christ. Christ has already borne the punishment for us, so even obvious sinners like the woman in this story can find a safe haven in the church. Exploring this story is not only a good practice of methods of Bible study but it also will inform your discussions about the character of the church.

2 Timothy 3:14-17

In 2 Timothy 3:10-17, the writer is concerned that the faithful not be misled by what he calls impostors. In the first-century Christian world there was a growing movement called gnosticism (NOS-tuh-siz-uhm). Paul and the leaders of the early church considered the teachings of this new movement inconsistent with the teachings of Christ and a threat to the blossoming Christian churches. Some of the gnostic heresies of the day included a strong belief that Christ's resurrection signaled the end times. This belief led to stringent fasting and celibacy in some and a "we're already saved so we can do what we want" attitude in others. The gnostics also held a belief in the godliness of Jesus that led to a rejection of Christ's suffering. Perhaps most offensive of all to the early Christians was a belief that those who ascribed to this gnostic gospel were somehow more enlightened and in tune with God's knowledge than other Christians.

The author of Timothy confronted these influences by challenging the church to remember its history and heritage. The truth he claimed lay in the sacred writings and the words and teachings of Jesus Christ.

The Greek word for *inspired* means literally "God-breathed" and appears only in this one passage in all of Scripture. This means that just as God breathed life into humankind, so also God somehow breathed life into these Scriptures to make them holy and inspired.

When discussing the author's caution to follow the Scriptures, it is important to remember that he would have been referring to the Old Testament, since Paul's body of letters were written well before the Gospel accounts and themselves were not collected into one body until much later.

The Canon

The Bible as we know it developed over many centuries. The Hebrew Scriptures that we call the Old Testament were passed down from generation to generation by storytelling around the campfire. It was not until around 1100 B.C. that they were recorded in any kind of written form, and then the writing materials were crude—stones and sheepskin. There were many more sacred books and stories than we have recorded in the Bible. The ones we have were selected over a period of time and were arranged into three groups—the Law, the Prophets, and the Writings. We know the Hebrew canon was set by the first century A.D. because in A.D. 98 at Jamnia, a council of respected rabbis and teachers reviewed the body of Scriptures called the Old Testament and removed some of the books. These are now part of the Apocrypha in most Protestant traditions.

The New Testament was finally set in the fourth century. The criteria for selecting books for the New Testament canon were: it had to be consistent with the teachings of Jesus, it had to be associated with an apostle, and it had to be widely used. Many books such as the Gospel of Thomas and the Shepherd of Hermas were not selected. The canon was closed at the end of the fourth century, and nothing has been added to it since. Some persons question whether this was a wise decision, for it implies that God stopped speaking to us and through us at that time.

---

1 Adapted from *Prayer and Temperament*, by Chester P. Michael and Marie C. Norrisey (Open Door, Inc., 1984); pages 50–51.

CHAPTER 6

GOD CALLS AND SENDS US

Learning Menu

Build your learning menu by selecting one or more learning ideas for each of the Learning Menu headings below:

1. to share personal feelings and memories about the church

2. to see the church as the body of Christ

3. to explore the purposes of the church

4. to close the session

AS THEY ENTER

☐A. WORSHIP AREA
—You will need a globe, bread, and grape juice.
—Place the globe and the elements for Holy Communion—bread
and grape juice—on the worship table, in addition to the candle and
Bible.

☐B. DOODLE SHEET
—You will need a large piece of paper and markers.
—Before the session, draw an outline of a church building on the
large piece of paper. Inside the outline, write a word or phrase that
means the church to you.
—As members of the group arrive, encourage them to write inside
the outline a word or phrase that means the church to them.

☐C. DEBRIEF ASSIGNMENT
—Ask: Were you able to study the Scriptures on the church during
the week?
  • Which Bible study approach did you use? Or, did you try both?
  • Did any new insights about the church occur to you from using
these methods?
  • Is this type of Bible study something you could find useful on a
regular basis? Why or why not?

LEARNING IDEA SELECTIONS

1. To share personal feelings and memories about the church.

☐A. OPENING DEVOTIONS
—Sing or read together the words of the hymn "We Are the
Church," using the words found on page 63 of the study book.
—Use the "Doodle Sheet" phrases to form a litany. Ask group mem-
bers to say "Thank you, God, for the church" after each word or
phrase you read from the Doodle Sheet.

☐B. REMEMBER THE CHURCH
—Ask the group members to sit comfortably, to close their eyes, and
to take three deep breaths to relax. Tell them to try to put all the
busyness of the day out of their minds and to just concentrate on
their breathing.
—Then ask them to go back through their memory tapes to their ear-
liest recollection of church. Have them call up that memory and
review it on the screen of their mind, feeling all the feelings,
smelling all the smells, hearing all the sounds of that first experience
with the body of Christ called the church.
—Allow them to enjoy that memory for three to five minutes. Then
ask them to return to the classroom by opening their eyes.
—Form the group members into teams. All those whose first memory
was of a worship service go to one corner; all those whose first memory was of Sunday school go to another corner; all those whose first
memory was of a youth event go to another; and anyone whose first
encounter was a funeral, camp meeting, or other such event go to
the fourth corner of the classroom.
—Ask team members to tell about their first experience of church.

• Was it a positive experience?
• Or was it a negative encounter?
• What people influenced their faith lives?
• What has brought them back to the church or kept them in the church to this day?
• Are there times when they have felt rejected by the church?

2. To see the church as the body of Christ.

☐A. FIND OUR PLACE IN THE BODY
—You will need masking tape and a large clear area of floor space.
—Before the session, make a large figure of a person on the floor with masking tape.
—Read aloud 1 Corinthians 12:12-31.
—Then ask group members to go to the part of the body they believe they are fulfilling in the body of Christ (the church) right now.
—Discuss: Why did you choose that part?
• Are you content to be there?
• Where would you rather serve?
• Do Paul's words confirm you or condemn you?
• How does our church recognize people's gifts and assimilate new members into the life of the church?
• What are some ways we could be doing that better?

☐B. STUDY THE BIBLE
—Divide the group members into teams of three or four persons to use the Ignatian Contemplation Approach to Bible Study (see page 37 of this leader's guide).
—Ask them to close their eyes and to relax by taking three deep breaths.
—Then read Matthew 16:13-18, asking them to place themselves in the person of one of the characters in the story as you read.
—Read the passage a second time, asking group members to take the role of a different character.
—After a moment or two of silence, ask members to open their eyes and to discuss their experience in their team, using the following questions:
• Which characters did you become?
• What insights about the church of Jesus Christ did you have?
• Who are the rocks in our church?
• What characteristics make these persons a rock?
• What are the values of membership in Christ's body, the church?
• What are the responsibilities of church membership?

3. To explore the purposes of the church.

☐A. EXPERIENCE CHURCH AS A CARING PLACE
—You will need plain white paper and pencils or pens.
—Give members a piece of plain white paper and a pen or pencil.
—Ask them to draw a line dividing their paper in half.
—Tell them to write "What I Need From the Church" on the top of the left side of the paper and to write "What I Can Give to the Church" on the top of the right side.
—Then ask them to list as many things as they can in each column.

—When they have finished, discuss: Which list is longer and why?
  • How can we make the church a more caring place for new people?
  • What can we do to reach out to people who are hurting?
  • How do we share our burdens in the church?

☐B. EXPERIENCE CHURCH AS A PLACE TO SERVE
—You will need to find out about some ecumenical service projects in your community or a nearby city, such as food pantries, soup kitchens, clothes closets, or Meals on Wheels. (Perhaps your pastor or the chairperson of your church's committee on church and society or social work can give you this information.) Make a list of the projects.
—Call the attention of the group members to the list of service projects. Ask: How many of you have participated in any of these projects?
  • Would you be interested in visiting some of these projects?
  • Would you be interested in planning a day you could volunteer to work at one of these projects?
—Be sure to follow-up, and plan a trip as soon as possible.

☐C. PRACTICE RANDOM ACTS OF KINDNESS
—Read the section "We Believe in the Reign of God . . . and in the Family of God," page 60 of the study book.
—Discuss the questions in the "Pause for Reflection" on page 61 of the study book.
—Brainstorm some ways group members could practice random acts of kindness.
—Make an assignment to try at least one of these ideas during the coming week.

☐D. EXPLORE THE CHURCH'S SACRAMENTS
—Discuss with the group members the meaning and history of the two sacraments—baptism and Holy Communion. (See the "Bible Background" for this chapter, page 44 of this leader's guide; and the box on page 59 of the study book.)
—Or, invite your pastor to attend this portion of the session. Ask him or her to lead a discussion of the sacraments and to officiate at a closing Communion service.
—Discuss: How do you feel about the sacraments?
  • What questions do you have about their significance, procedures, and so forth?
  • What do you understand about how the common elements of bread and grape juice become for us the body and blood of Christ?
  • How does the act of Communion fill us with the power of the Holy Spirit?
  • How often do you like to receive Communion? (Once a month? Every Sunday? Six times a year?) (Remind the group members that the early church observed Communion as part of their feasting together every time they met.)

4. To close the session.

☐A. SING A HYMN
—Sing or read together the words of "We Are the Church" (page 63 in the study book).

—You will need a large piece of paper and a marker.
—Explain that another major responsibility of the church is to pray for one another. We call these intercessory prayers.
—Ask group members to name their prayer concerns. List these concerns (people, crises, events, catastrophes) on the large piece of paper.
—Then pray for these people or items one at a time using the refrain "Lord in your mercy, hear our prayers" between each petition.

BIBLE BACKGROUND

Matthew 16:13-18

Caesarea Philippi was an interesting place for Christ to make his first announcement about his church. Caesarea Philippi was built by Herod's son Philip in honor of Caesar and himself. It was truly a pagan city, the site of one of the oldest shrines to the Greek god Pan—half man, half horse, and totally hedonistic in his worldly desires. With this backdrop Jesus asked the question: "Who do people say that [I am]?" Even though Jesus asked the question in this way, he was not concerned with other people but with his own disciples. Simon answered for himself and his fellow disciples: "You are the Messiah, the Son of the living God." Even as he said this, Jesus confirmed that this knowledge was not from Peter's head, his "flesh and blood"; the faith to which he was testifying was a gift from God. Although this passage has been interpreted as giving Peter the authority as leader of the future church, it has been suggested that the revelation from God and not the person of Peter is the rock upon which Christ builds his church.

Because Simon has the faith and courage necessary to warrant such a revelation, Jesus changes Simon's name to *Peter*, which means "rock." The word *rock* would have had significance for the disciples in that it was from a rock in the wilderness that Moses called forth a spring of water. They would remember that Moses was rebuked for claiming credit for that act, for that too was the revelation of God and not the result of human effort. Peter was not the chosen one; all those who believe in Jesus as the Messiah are the chosen.

Jesus was offering his followers a community that had not been spoken of before—the church, a unified family of believers. The Greek word for church is only used twice in the Gospels—here and Matthew 18:17. "On this rock I will build my church" extends to all the faithful believers down through the centuries who carry on the message and mission of Jesus Christ after he has gone to be with God in heaven.

1 Corinthians 12

Paul's letter to the church at Corinth was written to a largely Gentile congregation. Most of these Christians would have been poor and uneducated, probably many working as slaves and servants. There were many divisions in the church at Corinth because of a clash of leadership—Paul, Peter, and Apollo are all mentioned as having their own following.

Apparently Paul, during his time in Corinth, was prone to using ecstatic language also called "tongues" or "angel language" (1 Corinthians 13:1). Those who were able to do this began to feel that they were superior to others because they possessed this gift. Paul was squashing this misconception and affirming that there may indeed be more useful gifts like teaching and preaching. He affirmed that everyone has a gift to bring and all are needed to build the church.

In this passage Paul begins to develop his image of the church as the body of Christ in the world, and so he relates the metaphor to the human body. Also present in this chapter is Paul's reference to baptism as the initiation rite into the church. The phrase "baptized into one body—Jews or Greeks, slaves or free" recalls the baptismal formula of Galatians 3:27-28: "There is no longer Jew or Greek, there is no longer slave or free, there is no longer male and female; for all of you are one in Christ Jesus." Paul's total inclusion of all people is still a model for the church.

The Sacraments

God's self-giving love for all of creation and especially for us as God's children has been a recurring theme throughout this study as it has been a recurring theme throughout human history. This self-giving love reached its peak in the first century A.D. when God sent the Son to live among us, to teach us, and to model for us that self-giving love to the point of sacrificing his own life. Jesus said, "No one has greater love than this, to lay down one's life for one's friends" (John 15:13). God's self-giving did not stop with that great event, however. It continues to be poured out on us in grace that allows us to live without guilt, in unconditional love that challenges us to love and to forgive as well.

We preach and hear God's words through the Holy Scriptures, and we feel God's empowering presence through prayer and worship. But certain acts that we perform during worship in the community we call the church are particularly powerful vehicles through which we feel God's self-giving love and presence. Actions often speak louder than words; so Christ gave us two precious actions by which he promises we shall always feel God's presence. Those two actions we call sacraments or sacred acts. They are baptism and Holy Communion.

Baptism is the initiation into the Christian faith. For many it occurs as an infant, for others it occurs as an adult ready to commit one's life to God. Either way, baptism is an outpouring of God's love and also involves vows of faith and commitment. In infant baptism, the parents and the congregation vow to raise this child in the faith, protect him or her from temptation, and encourage and nurture the child to make her or his own commitment in adulthood. For adults, this act takes on a cleansing significance. New life

begins the day of baptism. All sins are washed away in the water of baptism—whether it be sprinkled, poured, or the person is immersed.

The water of baptism is first blessed by the minister, and the Holy Spirit is called to be present as it was at Jesus' own baptism in the river Jordan. As persons experience the water, they are (especially in immersion) believed to be dying like Christ and resurrected into new life with their rising from the water. Many denominations commemorate this belief by robing the baptized in white garments, as a symbol of purity. God's forgiveness washes over us with the water of baptism, and we begin a new way of life in Christ.

Because baptism is an initiation into the faith, most denominations believe that it should happen only once. The forgiveness continues to be experienced throughout our lives without having to feel the water again. However, our commitment may be forgotten. Thus, many denominations have services for the reaffirmation of the vows of baptism.

The Synoptic Gospels attest to the significance of Communion as not only a remembrance of Christ's blood and flesh being poured out for us but also as a mystical union with the Spirit of Christ that comes with the prayer of institution before Communion. For Roman Catholics, those words of prayer that invoke the power of the Holy Spirit actually change the wine and bread to the blood and body of Christ. For Protestants, the linkage is not so clear-cut. We believe that God infuses the common elements of bread and grape juice with a special power that allows us to feel Christ's presence in them and through them. We believe that the blessed juice and bread can literally fill us with the power of God's Holy Spirit as Christ promised. We also believe that by sharing this meal, we are joined together with Christians all over the world and in all centuries through Christ's timeless love for all humanity.

The act of Holy Communion is a solemn moment, but it is also a joyous one. Even as we remember Jesus' bitter, painful death, we also celebrate his victory over death for himself and for us.

In the sacred acts of baptism and Communion, we glimpse eternity.

CHAPTER 7

GOD GIVES US VICTORY

Learning Menu

Build your learning menu by selecting one or more learning ideas for each of the Learning Menu headings below:

1. to share life's tragedies

2. to understand that God is good despite the tragedies

3. to practice trust

4. to catch a glimpse of everlasting life

5. to evaluate the study and the learnings that have taken place

6. to close the session

AS THEY ENTER

☐ A. WORSHIP AREA
—You will need a plant, a picture of the Ascension, and a cross. If you are planning on closing with the anointing service, you will need a small container of olive oil mixed with a little natural scent perfume.
—Place the plant, cross, and picture of the Ascension on the worship table, along with the candle and Bible.

☐ B. DOODLE SHEET
—You will need a large piece of paper and colored markers.
—Before the session, write "What Color Is Hope?" in the center of the large piece of paper.
—As the members of the group arrive, direct them to the Doodle Sheet, and ask them to be creative in answering the question.

☐ C. DEBRIEF ASSIGNMENT
—Ask: Did anyone commit some random acts of kindness this week?
 • How do you feel about them?
 • How were they received?

LEARNING IDEA SELECTIONS

1. To share life's tragedies.

☐ A. READ A TRAGIC STORY
—Read the story of Michael Jordan, found on page 66 of the study book.
—Form teams of three or four persons, and discuss the questions in the "Pause for Reflection" on page 67 of the study book.

☐ B. FIND TRAGEDIES AROUND US
—You will need enough newspapers to give each group member a copy.
—Give group members a newspaper, and ask them to find some tragedies in the news.
—Form teams of three or four persons. Ask them to report on the tragedies they have found and to discuss the following questions:
 • Why does the newspaper print more tragic stories than hopeful ones?
 • What does this say about our society or about human nature?
 • Are there any evidences of God at work in the world in the newspaper?
 • How could God turn the tragedies into stories of hope and resurrection?
—Read the story on page 65 of the study book.
—Discuss: Where did this woman find hope?
 • Do you have that kind of hope in your own life? Why or why not?
 • Do Jesus' suffering and death give you hope when you are in crisis? If so, how?

2. To understand that God is good despite the tragedies.

☐ A. TELL A STORY
—Tell the following story:

God Is Good
 Two men set out on a journey together. They took a donkey to carry their packs, a torch to light their way at night, and a rooster, who was a friend of the donkey. The rooster sat on the donkey's head during the entire journey.

One of the men was deeply religious; the second was a skeptic. On the journey they frequently spoke about the Lord. "In all things, God is good," said the first companion.

"We will see if your opinion bears out on the trip," said the second.

Shortly before dusk the two men arrived in a small village where they sought a place to sleep. Despite their frequent requests, no one offered them a night's lodging. Reluctantly, they traveled a mile outside of town, where they decided to sleep.

"I thought you said God is good," the skeptic said sarcastically.

"God has decided this is the best place for us to sleep tonight," replied his friend.

They fixed their beds beneath a large tree, just off the main road that led to the village, tethering the donkey about 30 yards away. Just as they were about to light the torch they heard a horrible noise. A lion had killed the donkey and carried it off to eat it away from the two men. Quickly the two companions climbed the tree to stay away from danger.

"You still say God is good?" the skeptic asked with anger.

"If the lion hadn't eaten the donkey, he would have attacked us. God is good," his companion declared.

Moments later a cry from the rooster sent them further up the tree. From this new vantage point they saw a wildcat carrying the cock away in his teeth.

Before the skeptic could say a word, the man of faith declared, "The cry of the rooster has once again saved us. God is good."

A few minutes later a strong wind arose and blew out the torch, the only comfort of the men in the black night. Again the skeptic taunted his companion. "It appears that the goodness of God is working overtime this evening," he said. This time the believer was silent.

The next morning the two men walked back into the village for food. They soon discovered that a large band of outlaws had swept into town the previous night and robbed the entire village of all its possessions.

With this news the man of faith turned to his friend. "Finally it has become clear," he cried. "Had we been given a room in the village last night, we would have been robbed along with all of the villagers. If the wind had not blown out our torch, the bandits who traveled the road near the place where we slept would have discovered us and taken all our goods. It is clear, that in all things, God is good."[1]

—Discuss:
• How do you interpret the story?
• Is God always good?
• Can you give some experiences from your life of God's goodness, even in the midst of tragedy and challenge?

3. To practice trust.

☐A. GO ON A TRUST WALK
—You will need pieces of scrap material or scarves long enough to be used as blindfolds.
—Ask each group member to find a partner he or she trusts.
—Give each pair a blindfold, and let them decide who will be the leader and who will be blindfolded.
—Explain that the persons who are blindfolded are to depend on their partner to take them on a walk around the church.

—When each pair has completed their walk, have them change places and try the walk again.
—Discuss: Where was it easy and where was it difficult to trust?
   • Where is it easy and where is it difficult to trust God?
—Affirm that total trust is hard for all of us, and it is OK to be honest about your feelings.
—Turn to page 65 of the study book and read "We Believe in the Final Triumph of Righteousness."
—Discuss: How much did Jesus trust God in order to do all he did?
   • Is there anywhere in the Gospels where we see that it was hard for Jesus to trust? If so, how did he solve his problem? (See Matthew 26:36-46 and/or Mark 15:33-39; Luke 23:44-49.)

☐ B. READ KRISTIN'S STORY
—Turn to page 70 of the study book, and read the section "Trusting God."
—Discuss the issue of trust in this story.
   • Where did Kristin find her trust in Jesus and eternal life?
   • Are children better able to trust than adults? Why or why not?

4. To catch a glimpse of everlasting life.

☐ A. BIBLE STUDY
—Read the Resurrection story in Luke 24:1-12.
—Discuss: Do you believe this story completely?
   • What parts do you have questions about?
—Then read "God Is Good," page 67 of the study book.
—Discuss: How does this story explain Christ's gift of resurrection and how it requires our total trust?
   • Can we accept this free gift?
—Form teams of two or three persons. Ask the teams to talk about how the story of the Resurrection changes their life.

☐ B. SHARE RESURRECTION STORIES
—Read the section "We Believe in . . . the Life Everlasting," page 71 of the study book.
—Ask group members to share personal stories of death and resurrection.
—Discuss the "Pause for Reflection" questions on page 72 of the study book.

☐ C. CREATE A RESURRECTION EXPERIENCE
—You will need flower seeds, spoons, and a cup filled with dirt for each group member.
—Using spoons, allow each person to plant his or her seeds.
—As group members work, remind them that unless a seed falls into the ground and is buried, it cannot bring forth flowers or fruit (see John 12:24).
—Each group member will have a "cup of new life," a new plant, to take home as a reminder of God's gift of eternal life.

5. To evaluate the study and the learnings that have taken place.

☐ A. REWRITE YOUR CREED
—You will need the creeds the group members wrote during the first session.
—Return the creeds the group members wrote during the Introductory Session.